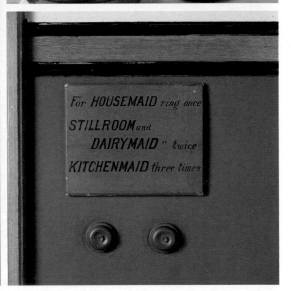

Lanhydrock

Cornwall

Paul Holden

National Trust

Window on a vanished world

LANHYDROCK is presented at its late Victorian and Edwardian zenith, when it was the family home of Thomas, 2nd Lord Robartes, his wife Mary and their ten children, who were looked after by a staff of 80. The rooms you see today were largely created after a devastating fire in 1881 had severely damaged much of the house. Lord Robartes instructed his architects, Richard Coad and James MacLaren, to rebuild in a traditional Jacobean style, but according to a strict Victorian moral code, which segregated public and private areas, master and servant, young and old, male and female. Every function was given its own room – from Nursery Scullery to Lamp Room, Meat Larder to Prayer Room. Lanhydrock's Victorian kitchens, nursery suite and staff quarters remain among the best pre-served in Britain, offering a fascinating insight into a lost world, both above and below stairs.

Never again

Not surprisingly, Lord Robartes was anxious to prevent another fire. For this reason, neither gas nor electricity was installed. The new ceilings were constructed, not of conventional wooden beams, but of fireproof reinforced concrete twelve inches thick. A huge reservoir was buried deep in the higher gardens to supply water to the house and to the new fire hydrants installed by James Merryweather & Sons.

The Jacobean house

But Lanhydrock is far more than just a Victorian home. The house, garden and estate, situated in the densely wooded valley of the River Fowey near Bodmin, have remained in the ownership of a single family since around 1621, with each generation making its own significant alter-ations.

Lanhydrock is essentially a 17th-century house, largely the creation of John Robartes, who became 1st Earl of Radnor in 1679. The best-preserved parts of his house are the Gatehouse and the Gallery, with its superb plasterwork ceiling and important library.

Key figures

John Robartes, later 1st Earl of Radnor, created the Jacobean house with its superb plasterwork and Gatehouse.

Anna Maria Agar (née Hunt) revived Lanhydrock in the early 19th century by restoring the house and creating an exciting garden and surrounding landscape.

'Little Lordy': Thomas, 2nd Lord Robartes rebuilt Lanhydrock after the fire of 1881. His affectionate nickname referred to his diminutive stature.

Michael Trinick, the National Trust's Regional Director for Cornwall, revived the neglected house and conceived the innovative presentation of the servants' quarters.

(Above) Captain Tommy's Dressing Room

Successive Earls of Radnor preferred to live outside Cornwall, neglecting the house, while relying on the income generated by the estate. It was their descendants, George Hunt and his niece Anna Maria Hunt, owners from 1758, who revived the place.

Saving Lanhydrock

Lanhydrock is lucky to have survived into the 21st century, as history reveals a house often ill at ease with its unfashionable architecture and isolated position. It was considered for demolition, first in 1754 and again in 1881. Its fortunes declined further as the family diminished throughout the 20th century. When the National Trust accepted the property in 1953, it did so for the landscape value of the park and estate; the house was considered a white elephant.

The acquisition and presentation of the house today is a testament to the commitment and enthusiasm of the late Michael Trinick, the National Trust's Regional Director for Cornwall, who worked tirelessly towards interpreting Lanhydrock as the late Victorian home of the Agar-Robartes family.

> 'Lanhydrock shows a way of life which in most houses had come to an end by 1914.'
>
> Michael Trinick

3

Tour of the House

The Gatehouse

The Gatehouse was built in 1651 as a hunting lodge. The first-floor chamber would have been a popular position from which to follow the deer-hunt and survey the kill. A 17th-century drawing shows a small cupola on the roof (long since gone), which would have offered picturesque views over the garden and park. Architecturally, the outward façade of the Gatehouse displays the vibrancy of the Italian Renaissance with fashionable columns and arches, although the inward-looking elevation was modelled in a more traditional Gothic style.

By 1799 the hunting lodge was known as the Porter's Lodge, a fireplace being inserted to create a modicum of comfort. Soon afterwards, when the parkland swept up to the front of the house, the building served as a charming isolated folly before becoming a useful and delightful entrance feature in 1858, when the formal gardens were laid out. Throughout the late 19th century, the first floor of the Gatehouse was used as a Sunday school for the parish, and during the Second World War it functioned as a Catholic chapel for evacuees (see p. 56).

The Exterior

The North Range (right of entrance)

This predates the rest of the house and survived the fire almost unscathed. As the granite blocks used here are similar in size to those on the church, it probably once formed part of the medieval priory buildings, perhaps a barn or priory grange. In the mid-16th century it was probably the original Barton farmhouse.

John Robartes, who succeeded his father as Baron Robartes in 1634, inserted the doorway (today leading into the Shop) marked '1636: ILR: L' (1636: John Lord Robartes: Lanhydrock)

The Gatehouse and entrance front

in order to create a more fashionable cross-passage house. From 1636 John embarked on an ambitious building programme that made Lanhydrock one of the most impressive mansions in the south-west.

The West Range (entrance range)

It was completed between 1636 and 1640, with the arms of the Robartes family on display above the front door. By the end of the 18th century the external granite walls had been painted red, presumably to imitate the contemporary fashion for red brick. As soon as Anna Maria Hunt inherited the house, she instructed her steward, William Jenkin, to remove the paint:

I am sorry to find the red paint cannot be got off from the old house at Lanhydrock so completely as to restore the walls to the original colour ... although they washed the stones with Hot Water and soap.

Instead, she asked that the walls be repainted in yellow to resemble Portland stone. Evidence of this colour can still be seen on this range and on the Gatehouse – it is particularly noticeable after heavy rain. During George Gilbert Scott's mid-19th-century work, the windows on the façade were fitted with plate glass. The leaded lights as seen today were installed in more recent times.

The South Range (left of entrance)

This was originally completed in 1642 – the date is carved above the blind door that once led into the Brewhouse (now the Billiard Room). After the fire a full restoration of this range was intended, as Richard Coad's first contract plans show. Coad later wrote to impress on Lord Robartes 'the serious effect the fire had on the walls.... [However,] what I have to combat is the feeling that I am destroying more than I should do – this is far from my desire'. Reluctantly, he rebuilt the South Range to make it structurally sound and to redesign the functional living space inside. The architect created a maze of corridors and stairs, laid out around two internal courtyards, providing new service rooms that in turn created a fully segregated environment. On the ground floor, the Kitchen and kitchen offices contained the

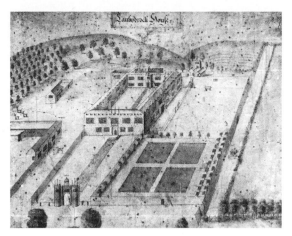

The house in the 17th century, showing the east range, which was demolished about 1784

latest devices for cooking, hygiene and storage. In addition, numerous preparation areas, baking and dairy rooms with larders for fish and meat afforded convenience, modernity and efficiency. On the first floor, an extensive Nursery suite catered for a rapidly growing family, while the rooms above functioned as male and female staff accommodation.

An inscribed stone sits high up on this range with the mysterious initials 'S:B E:B'. These letters appear to have no relevance to the Victorian family nor their builders, so perhaps they copy a Jacobean inscription.

The East Range (demolished)

It contained the main reception rooms of the original 17th-century quadrangular building. In 1669 the Duke of York's Chief Treasurer, Thomas Povey, visited the house and remarked with some admiration: 'A stately fabric, my curious eye, Sparkles with uniformity'. In 1758 William Borlase, Rector of Ludgvan near Penzance, described the first floor as 'one large antechamber a handsome apartment communicating with the Gallery which is the length of the whole Eastern Front'. It formed a second gallery or 'Prospect Chamber' that gave extensive views east overlooking the deer-park. The East Range was removed c.1784 by George Hunt to create a more fashionable, yet still symmetrical, 'E'-shaped house.

The Interior

The Porch

The two entrance doors to the house set the tone for the architectural styles that lie beyond. The 17th-century panelled front door, heavily carved in oak, displays the heraldic devices of the 1st Baron Robartes and remains a resolute reminder of the family's Jacobean ancestry. The inner door was remade after the fire in the Arts and Crafts style, which sought to reform industrial design through the revival of handicrafts.

The Outer Hall

The restful tone of this room echoes its 17th-century use as a hall. In the 1950s and '60s the last generation of the Agar-Robartes family would meet here before going in to dinner. Family photographs are on the table by the front door.

Many of the original features survived the fire, such as the robust granite *fireplace*, some of the *plasterwork frieze* and much of the *oak panelling*. Unfortunately, the Jacobean wooden screens passage that ran across the width of the room was destroyed – only a pair of caryatids (carved figures used as architectural columns or supports), now on display in the Gallery, was saved.

The low geometric *ceiling* was crafted in 1883 by the Davy brothers of Pensilva, a village on the edge of Bodmin Moor. All of the decorated Victorian ceilings in the house mimic those of the original 17th-century house. The *double doors* at the far end lead directly on to the Grand Staircase, which connected with the withdrawing chambers above.

Pictures

On the wall above the radiator are portraits of *Thomas James Agar-Robartes, 1st Baron Robartes (1808–82)* and his wife *Juliana Pole-Carew, Lady Robartes (1812–81)* by George Richmond RA

The 17th-century front door

(1809–96). Between these is *John Robartes, 4th Earl of Radnor (1686–1757),* grandson of the 1st Earl. He did not inherit Lanhydrock and lived at Radnor House in Twickenham near the poet Alexander Pope. On the left of the fireplace are two circular portraits in the manner of Cornelius Johnson (1593–1661). The first, a copy of the full-length portrait on the Oak Staircase, shows *Sir Richard Robartes, 1st Baron Robartes of Truro (c.1580–1634)*. Alongside is his wife *Frances Hender (d. 1626)*, daughter of John Hender of Boscastle, Cornwall. To the right of the double doors is a childhood full-length portrait of *Henry Robartes, 3rd Earl of Radnor (c.1695–1741)*. In 1754 his sister Mary Vere suggested that Henry had paid out £400 on furniture for Lanhydrock – a substantial amount for the early 18th century. On the far wall is a portrait of *John Robartes, 1st Earl of Radnor (1606–85)* by Sir Godfrey Kneller, Bt (1646/9–1723). Seen here in his robes as Lord Privy Seal, Robartes was fortunate to regain royal favour after his part in the Parliamentary revolt of 1642. Between the windows is *John Hunt of Mollington Hall*. John Hunt's son Thomas married into the Robartes family in 1719.

Leave by the double doors to the right of the fireplace and enter the cloakroom where we provide secure lockers for your use. Turn left into the Inner Hall.

Pictures

In the corridor is a large canvas by J.E.C. Mathews (1842–1927) dated 1880, showing the Prince of Wales leaving Brighton Hospital with a Sovereign's Escort of the Middlesex Yeomanry.

The Inner Hall

After the fire the Inner Hall was extended outwards from an existing corridor that linked the kitchens to the house. The durable *mosaic floor* was laid by 1884. Recent monitoring has shown recurring movement in the foundations, which has dislodged some of the marble tesserae and placed excessive pressure on both the staircases.

A solid-fuel *central-heating system* was installed at Lanhydrock in the mid-19th century, but this room, like many in the house, was first centrally heated by G. N. Haden & Sons during the restoration works. This Victorian system is still in use today, with the water being heated by natural gas and controlled by a building management system that maintains a constant humidity of 58 per cent in each room so that the delicate contents are protected.

The pattern of the William-Morris-style *wallpaper* is 'Seaweed'.

The daily *post* was collected from this area, as the letter-box dated 1873, stamp machine and weighing scales indicate. The large *thermometer* in the courtyard beyond could be illuminated by a switch in the window

(Right) The Outer Hall decorated for Christmas

embrasure. The **engraved glass** in the double doors, reminiscent of Victorian public houses, is an uncommon feature in domestic interiors and reflects the increasing awareness of oriental design during the late 19th century.

Pictures and sculpture

The charming pencil-and-wash paintings on easels are dated 1844 and signed by George Richmond RA (1809–96). The subjects are *Juliana Pole-Carew (1812–81)* of Antony in east Cornwall, who married *Thomas James Agar-Robartes (1808–82)* in 1839. Sadly, both died soon after the fire. The picture above the fireplace is by Robert Thornton, ARA (1818–85) and shows *Juliana Pole-Carew* at the time of her marriage. Above the radiator are portraits of *Thomas Charles Agar-Robartes, 6th Viscount Clifden (1844–1930)* and his wife *Mary Dickinson, Viscountess Clifden (1853–1921)* by Henry Weigall (1829–1925). The portrait bust is of *Henry Phillpotts, Bishop of Exeter (1778–1875),* by Henry William Pickersgill RA (1782–1878). This West-Country prelate created the Diocese of Truro and authorised the change from a perpetual curacy at Lanhydrock to a 'regular' parish at the request of Lord Robartes.

The Teak Bedroom Staircase

Beyond the Inner Hall is an impressive Elizabethan-style staircase made of teak that replaced a pre-fire staircase in the same position. James MacLaren's original, more fanciful designs were apparently much altered by Richard Coad to fit the plainer style requested by Lord Robartes.

Pictures and sculpture

At the foot of the Teak Bedroom Stairs are portraits by Edwin Long RA (1829–91) and Walter William Ouless RA (1848–1933) of the *6th Viscount and Viscountess Clifden*. Above the radiator is a portrait by John King (1788–1847) of the *Rev. Gerald Pole-Carew (1815–45)*, curate of Lanhydrock and brother of Juliana, Lady Robartes. A portrait bust of the local historian *Davies Gilbert MP, PRS (1767–1839)* by Sir Richard Westmacott (1775–1856) is displayed on the window-sill. On the wall is a print by Montbard of the *Fire at Lanhydrock House*. Published in the *Illustrated London News* nearly two weeks after the fire in April 1881, the image is an imaginative representation of events.

Return to the Inner Hall and pass through the double doors into the Dining Room.

The Dining Room

Like many Victorians, the Agar-Robartes family were influenced by French cuisine, with menus often being written in French. During the late 19th century, upper-class dining was governed by stiff ceremony that seems – to modern taste – more of an ordeal than a pleasure. Wines would have been served with each course. On 11 June 1950 a more informal luncheon was served here for King George VI and Queen Elizabeth during their tour of Cornwall.

Prior to the fire, this room was used as the Servants' Hall and later as the Gun Room and Housekeeper's Room. After the fire, it became the Dining Room, positioned facing east so as to be cooler in the evening.

Although essentially refurbished in the Jacobean style, the room draws on the popularity of High-Victorian Aesthetic design. Many features, in particular the **overmantel** and the plasterwork **ceiling**, are richly carved with naturalistic grapes and vines, while the deep-relief **carvings** throughout relate to food-and-drink themes. MacLaren specified heavily embossed Spanish leather hangings costing 50 shillings (£2.50) per roll. The William Morris green and gilt 'Sunflower' **wallpaper** is a modern copy, but suits the original intention.

Tableware

The *epergne* (table centrepiece) was presented to Lord and Lady Robartes by the miners of Redruth in 1869 in appreciation of their support for the Miners' Infirmary. Appropriately, it is made of Cornish tin rather than silver, which was more usual for such oasis scenes. The silver *comports* (shallow dishes) are by E. & J. Barnard, London, 1851–2. On the side-table is a bone china and gilt floral decorated **dessert service** made by Daniel & Sons, *c.*1820–40.

(Left) The Dining Room   (Right) The Servery

Pictures

The painting of *Francis Basset MP (1715–69)* by Thomas Gainsborough (1727–88) was given to the National Trust by the eminent Cornish historian A. L. Rowse. The Bassets from Tehidy, near Redruth, were staunch Royalists during the English Civil War, so would have considered the Robarteses as bitter enemies. However, the families were reconciled in 1920, when Victor Agar-Robartes, later 8th Viscount Clifden, married Patience Mary Basset at Westminster Abbey. Above the side-table is a portrait of *Thomas Hunt III (1721–88)* in the manner of Arthur Devis (1712–87).

The Servery

Conveniently placed between the Dining Room, China Cupboard, Kitchens and the Butler's Pantry, this was primarily used to keep food warm before serving. The room contains a large linen press and a steam-heated hot-cupboard supplied by Clement Jeakes & Co.

Proceed out of the Servery, turn right and then immediately left into the Butler's Passage. Turn right into the Kitchen Quarters and left into the main Kitchen.

The Kitchen Quarters

Before the fire, the kitchens were in their current position. However, the ancillary rooms such as the Brewhouse, Laundry, Servants' Hall and staff accommodation were located further east along the south range. The repairs of 1881 gave this High-Anglican family the opportunity to apply their strongly held moral codes to the design of the house. This resulted in the strict segregation of male and female quarters, both above- and below-stairs. The butler, housekeeper, housemaids and scullery-maids, for example, had their own specified doorways.

The sheer size of these kitchens, coupled with the introduction of the latest technology, indicates that they were built to impress. Yet, at the time of the fire the family had only three children and did not entertain on a lavish scale. After the death of the son and heir Tommy Agar-Robartes in 1915 and the departure of the other children, the household diminished and the kitchen offices gradually fell into disuse. Between the wars the original Clement Jeakes & Co. spit was replaced by conventional Agas, and the doors of the largely redundant kitchen offices were closed, with only the Meat Larder having any regular use.

In the 1970s the kitchens were first added to the visitor route, quickly establishing themselves as firm favourites.

In 2003 paint samples were taken from the walls and woodwork to determine the original 1884 colour schemes. These colours were reinstated and the kitchens reinterpreted, based on extensive new research, for the start of the 2005 season. These kitchens survive in outstanding condition and are amongst the finest Victorian domestic interiors in England.

The Kitchen

Coad designed this large room in the style of a college hall with a high-gabled roof and clerestory windows that open by shafted gears situated in the end dresser. The high windows kept out direct sunlight and allowed unpleasant smells and heat to escape. But when all the fires were in action, it must still have been almost unbearably hot. In 1884 the main kitchen was painted in a curious pink colour, but due to the heat and dirt generated, this was soon changed to a more practical butterscotch.

Equipment

The kitchen equipment was designed, supplied and installed by Clement Jeakes & Co. of Great Russell Street in London, which held Queen Victoria's Royal Warrant. The large *rotary spit*, turned by a fan in the chimney called a smoke-jack, allowed several cooking processes to be carried out at once. To achieve the best standards of food preparation, modern technology was used, with much of the equipment being powered by steam supplied from a generator in the cellar. Immediately to the left of the spit is a *steaming platform*, while to the right a second alcove once contained a *confectionery oven*. The *Biffault range* alongside the door to the Kitchen Scullery most likely replaced a Jeakes charcoal range in the early 20th century.

Several work stations are set up on the large *central table*. The *end dresser* holds copperware and ceramics, while the *dresser beneath the windows* contains crockery that needed to be readily to hand. Ham joints are hung on the *high rack* above the *batterie de cuisine*.

The staff's morning duties

5.30: Brush and clean kitchen ranges. Light fires and boil kettles.

6.30: Prepare Breakfast Room: clean grate, light fire, dust room and lay cloth for breakfast. Clean steps and polish brass. Fifteen-minute break to say prayers. Prepare staff breakfast and clear away.

8.00: Heat water and take to the bedrooms for the family to wash. Remove slops to Sluice Room. Lady's-maid and footman assist in dressing family.

9.15: Strip beds and tidy bedrooms, while family has breakfast.

10.30: Clear away and wash up breakfast things.

(Right) The Kitchen

The Kitchen Offices

To provide space for the new kitchen offices, dynamite was used to blast away the hill to the west of the house. Each of these rooms had its own precise function.

The Kitchen Scullery

This would have been a very busy room where fresh produce from the kitchen garden and game from the estate was received and prepared.

Immediately on the left is a *platform used for steaming* fish, meat and vegetables in large copper steaming pans. The *zinc-lined sink* was in constant demand for the endless washing-up that was generated by the main kitchen. The high-level *plate rack* provided out-of-the-way drying space.

At the opposite end of the room is a *slate sink* used for preparing vegetables. The wooden box by the door is a *hay-box*, used to keep food hot overnight either for the family or for shooting parties. The *range* would have been ideal for making jams and chutneys, although this would have also been carried out in the Housekeeper's Still Room. In front of the fireplace is a portable *heating cupboard* lined with tin to absorb the heat of the fire. The blue colour of the kitchen walls was believed to repel flies.

Leave by the far door, cross the porch and enter the Bakehouse.

The Kitchen Scullery

The Bakehouse

The porch entrance is cleverly positioned to eliminate unnecessary lifting of heavy vegetables, coal and flour through the kitchen. Here bread was made on a daily basis for family and staff. Three massive *dough troughs* stand underneath the window. Once the dough had

Carpet-beating at Lanhydrock

Staffing

In the period leading up to the First World War, approximately 80 staff were employed to maintain the house and estate, often recruited from nearby orphanages or the local community. The most senior staff were the butler and housekeeper, who directly represented the interests of his Lordship and her Ladyship. Together, they led a dedicated team, comprising: cook, governess, nanny, two maids, two nursery-maids, four housemaids, two kitchen-maids, scullery-maid, dairy-maid, still-room-maid, charwoman, three footmen, valet, odd-man, three chauffeurs, two coachmen, two grooms, gamekeeper, steward, land agent and pantry boy. The gardens and estate had a similar number of personnel, comprising: eleven gardeners, eleven general estate workers, nine Home Farm staff, six wood-men, two electricians and six general labourers. By 1939 the reduced household required only seventeen staff.

Wages were modest by our standards: the steward received £100–125 per year, while the estate labourers received just £1 4s (£1.20) for working a 50-hour week. Deductions were made for board, clothing and sustenance so that the housemaids, for example, took home only 5s (25p) a week. It was customary for married staff to live in a cottage on the estate, for which 1s (5p) a week was deducted as rent. The family had an exceptionally high regard for their staff, some of whom were employed at Lanhydrock through six generations. They would lay on a wedding breakfast for staff who got married and give presents at Christmas and birthdays.

been mixed and had risen, it was placed in tins, which were then put in the *lower proving oven* and, finally, baked in the *oven above*. The oven would have taken four days to reach an even temperature.

The Pastry Room

This section of the house was cut back into the hill above to provide a cool and dry environment for the next set of kitchen offices.

The *marble slab* under the window was for preparing and rolling pastry. Below are two *massive drawers* for storing flour. The *pestle and mortar* would have been used to break down the contents of the dry storage cupboard (often called a Pastry-Dresser) opposite or sugar from the large cone for use in cakes and biscuits. The *meat safe* by the door stored cooked meats.

(Right) The Pantry Room

The Pantry

This room contains cool *slate slabs* for storing cooked foods and *ice chests* for preparing ice-cream. Elaborately moulded ice-cream would have been made by the cook on a daily basis fresh for the table. Ice was an important element of the Victorian kitchen. As Lanhydrock had no ice-house on site, ice was brought by train from Plymouth.

The Meat Larder

The danger of storing cooked meat alongside raw game was not appreciated by Robert Kerr, whose book, *A Gentleman's House* (1864), was used extensively by Coad in planning the Kitchen Quarters. In this room there is a game rack for hanging freshly killed birds alongside ceiling racks for cooked meats.

The Meat Larder was also used as a butchery (hence the large *butcher's block* in the corner), while the *dressing-tables* under the windows would have been used for trussing. The early *refrigerator*, which would have been packed with ice, stored raw fish. Alongside, eggs were limed in large glazed stoneware jars.

(Above) The Meat Larder
(Right) The Dairy

The Dairy Scullery

Milk was brought from Home Farm by pony cart and delivered to the outside door of the Dairy Scullery. The churns were emptied into pans which stood in the cold-water-filled *troughs* against the wall. Whole milk was set aside for household use, and the remainder used for making butter, cheese, clotted cream, curds and junkets. To make butter, cream was skimmed off the top of the milk after it had stood for 24 hours and was then worked in the *up-and-over tub*. In making clotted cream, the milk was warmed in ceramic pans on the *scalding range* against the wall. These were heated by hot-water pipes linked directly to the boiler house in the cellar below. The cool conditions were ideal for storing eggs.

The Dairy

This room was for storage and not preparation. On the same site as the north-facing Jacobean dairy, the room has elaborate Victorian cooling arrangements. The *slate runnels* and the central *marble slab* would have been flooded with piped spring water supplied from the hills above the house. Here cold puddings and dairy products, which were prepared well in advance, could be stored. The tiling was for hygiene: a William Morris-style tiled border made a modest concession to fashion.

Retrace your steps, returning through the Dairy Passage and Butler's Passage, turning right into the main house corridor.

The Corridor

The handsome Minton-tiled *pavement* is typical of the flooring advocated by Charles Eastlake in his book *Hints on Household Taste* (1868). Many of the post-fire interior features of Lanhydrock were influenced by Eastlake's writings. The *carpet* was made by the Woodward Grosvenor factory in Kidderminster. Although modern, it reflects an original design of 1884.

The family presented the *Agar-Robartes* lifeboat to the Lizard in 1863 at a cost of nearly £200. The *model* was given to Lord Robartes in 1867. The mahogany *longcase clock* with swan-neck pediment, *c*.1790, is inscribed on the dial 'Middleton, London'.

Pictures

The Funeral of Walter von Vogelweide by Friedrich Arnold (b.1814) is on the right wall opposite the Servery. Outside Lady Robartes's Sitting Room are two portraits: *Caroline Carey, c.1840*, mother of Mary Dickinson, later Viscountess Clifden, by an unkown artist, and her great-grandmother, *Phillippa Fuller,* by Francis Cotes RA (1726-70). These two paintings were bequeathed to the National Trust by Joy Burden, a descendant of the Dickinson family, in 2010. *An Italian man in a doublet and gorget* is a Victorian copy by Caroline Littleton of a 16th-century portrait. By the Nursery Stairs on the left-hand side is an English 19th-century portrait of *Reginald Yorke (1845-78)*. Yorke was related to the Earls of Hardwicke, who once owned Wimpole Hall.

Half-way along the corridor on the left is Lady Robartes's Sitting Room.

Lady Robartes's Sitting Room

After the family moved back into the house in 1885, many of the rooms changed their intended functions. Originally, this room was meant to be his Lordship's Sitting Room, but its proximity to the butler, cook, governess, housekeeper and nanny made it a more suitable place from which her Ladyship could conduct household business and plan her charity work.

Amongst the contents of this 'Briar Rose'-papered room are mementoes of Mary, Lady Robartes, including photographs of her childhood home, Kingweston in Somerset, watercolours of family members and pictures of family pets.

Continue along the Corridor, descend the stairs under the granite arch into the Lobby. Here the big game trophies introduce the masculine preserve common to most large late Victorian homes. Many of the photographs record the children's time at public school and university, including membership of the exclusive Bullingdon and Beefsteak clubs. On the left is the door to the Steward's Room.

The Steward's Room

At the time of the fire Silvanus Jenkin was the Lanhydrock agent or steward, as they were often called in the West Country. He was from a long line of Jenkins involved in the family fortunes for over 100 years. The room was carefully placed close to the service courtyard door so that

(Right)
The Billiard Room

(Opposite page)
The Steward's Room

tenants could enter the house, pay their rents, and leave without being seen.

On the wall is one of Lanhydrock's internal *telephones*. The house was connected to an external exchange in 1909. High on the wall are four of Richard Coad's *floor plans* for the post-fire restoration of the house. Much of the *furniture* in this room was transferred from another Lanhydrock estate office in Liskeard. On the shelves are *copy books*, which contain duplicates of all outgoing estate letters.

The Billiard Room

Prior to the 1860s the billiard-table was in the Gallery, while this room was used as the Brewhouse with a Laundry alongside. The 2nd Lord Robartes had a passion for the game, spending a good deal of time in billiard halls while a student at Christ Church, Oxford, in the 1850s. After the fire the Billiard Room became a focal point for male entertaining, especially during the political campaigns of Tommy Agar-Robartes (see p. 54). The Lanhydrock ladies also enjoyed the game.

The sumptuous *ceiling* and elaborate *fireplace* create the Jacobean style of this room, while the Arts and Crafts electric *light fittings* are of fine quality. The mahogany and slate-bedded *billiard table* was made by Burroughs & Watts. A radiator underneath the table heats the playing surface to the optimum level. Many different games may be played on a billiard-table. The rules of 'pyramids' are on display, while the scoreboard relates to a game called life pool. On the mantelpiece are commemorative *tankards* engraved especially for matches involving members of the Agar-Robartes family. Evacuees recall this room housing Viscount Clifden's train set during the Second World War.

This room also reflects the family's interest in *cricket*. The 1st Lord Robartes was the first Cornish member of the MCC (in 1827) and the first person in Cornwall to employ professional players. Cricket was played in the park at Lanhydrock. Later, a purpose-built cricket ground was laid out beside the present car-park.

Return, turn left and pass the steps to the Smoking Room.

The Smoking Room

The Smoking Room

The Arts-and-Crafts-style chimneypiece, dated 1883 on the side, is typical of James MacLaren's progressive design work in the house. The glass-fronted cabinet was designed to hold a decanter. We can only speculate on the political conversations held in this room during the visits of such Liberal Party luminaries as W. E. Gladstone, H. H. Asquith, Winston Churchill, Lord Rosebery and the Marquess of Crewe.

Many of the pictures in the room depict horsemanship – another great passion of the Agar-Robartes family. The *pin or 'pop' boards* crossed with canes were brought back from Tommy Agar-Robartes's study at Eton. On the window-sill to the left, the young Tommy Agar-Robartes mischievously carved his initials.

We can only wonder what his father's reaction was!

Return up the steps and ascend the staircase on the left. At the top, turn right into the bedroom corridor. If you are unable to use the stairs, a lift is available. Please ask for assistance.

'The pitiable resources to which some gentlemen are driven in order to be able to enjoy the pestiferous luxury of a cigar, have given rise to the occasional introduction of an apartment specially dedicated to the use of Tobacco.'

Robert Kerr, *The Gentleman's House* (1864)

The Nursery Staircase

At the top of the stairs are two pictures in the style of Sir Godfrey Kneller depicting *The Hon. Francis Robartes MP (c.1650–1718),* and his first wife, *Penelope Pole,* a member of the Pole family who later succeeded to Antony House in Cornwall. Francis Robartes, son of the 1st Earl of Radnor, was a composer and became Vice-President of the Royal Society.

Turn right into the corridor and then left into Captain Tommy's Dressing Room.

Captain Tommy's Dressing Room and Bedroom

In 1886 these rooms were being used as children's bedrooms, one for Tommy and the other probably for his twin sister Everilda. Today, they show the personal arrangements of Tommy Agar-Robartes, the heir to a Cornish estate of some 70,000 acres, whose life was tragically cut short during the Great War of 1914–18.

The dressing room was a private sitting room to offer some seclusion in a busy household.

Perhaps the most personal item in the bedroom is a copy of the New Testament inscribed 'T.C. A–R 1914'. The walls are hung with personal mementoes of Tommy's curtailed life. The three oil paintings are a landscape by Benjamin Barker of Bath (1776–1838) dated 1811, *Truro Churchyard from Kenwyn* by Garstin Cox (1892–1933), and *A Girl with a Violin* painted by Harewood Robinson (active 1884–96).

Continue out of the bedroom, into the Bay Bedroom corridor. On your left is the Family Museum which displays some of Lanhydrock's great treasures

An 1897 photograph on the wall shows the nine Agar-Robartes children. The brass rods were inserted in the stair balustrades to stop the young children falling through, perhaps while they eavesdropped on the political conversations below.

Tommy's dressing case was returned to the family after his death at the Battle of Loos in 1915. Made of crocodile skin with leather fitments by Asprey's & Sons of London, the case contains fully monogrammed silver-topped bottles, ivory accessories and walnut cases. Some of the bottles contain the original tooth and talcum powders used by Tommy, while one of the walnut containers has the rouge that he would have put on his cheeks to mask the ashen greyness caused by fear in the trenches.

The Nursery Suite

With a growing family, the Agar-Robarteses recognised the need to enlarge the Jacobean house, and the fire of 1881 provided the opportunity to add a self-contained nursery suite. The nursery rooms are south-facing so that they remain light and airy with a sunny prospect and are adequately insulated by the service rooms above and below. In addition, they are positioned far from the Drawing Room, where the family entertained. During the Second World War these rooms housed evacuees from London (see p. 56). In later years they functioned as a self-contained flat for a member of the clergy.

The Day Nursery

The Nursery Scullery

This was used by the nanny or nursery-maids. As specified by Kerr, it was near the Day Nursery. Just outside the Scullery is a Swiss-made wooden *cuckoo clock* of *c.*1800. Like many items in the house, it was given to the National Trust by the 7th Viscount Clifden.

The Nursery Scullery

The Day Nursery

This room was occupied throughout the day by the children, while in the evening the nanny would have used it as her sitting room to while away what little spare time she had. The fireplace cleverly incorporates mirrors placed at head height for the children.

The room contains a fine collection of toys, many of which once belonged to the Agar-Robartes children. The impressive *doll's house* dates from about 1902. To the left of the door is a late Victorian Kirkman Patented Improved Trichord upright *piano*. The *rocking horse* is early 19th-century.

The Night Nursery

Mary and Thomas Charles Agar-Robartes had ten children between 1879 and 1895. Of these, one, John Radnor (b. 1884), died in infancy. At any one time this room accommodated three or four of the younger children until they were ready to move into bedrooms of their own. This room has a comforting *fireplace* and a large *fireguard* on which to dry clothes. The wood used throughout the Nursery is pine, painted with a grain effect to simulate oak.

In the corner is a fine collection of Victorian children's books, many inscribed by parents to their children.

Nanny's Room

The hierarchy of staff in a house of this size was of great importance. Few would have had personal contact with the family. Nanny was one exception, taking direct instruction from the lady of the house. This room contained her personal effects and as such was regarded as her own personal space. However, it would have been considered normal that the youngest child would have slept alongside Nanny.

The Nursery Bathroom

The bathroom, one of only two installed in the house after 1881, was placed here for convenience. The *hanging* over the bath is in the style of the Aesthetic Movement.

Turn left into the Nursery Corridor past the Schoolroom and then cross the Bedroom Corridor to the Men's Stone Staircase.

Nanny's Room

The Men's Stone Staircase

Robert Kerr wrote, 'The family constitute one community, the staff another'. Nowhere is this more apparent than where the two sets of stairs lead from the house to the staff accommodation. The female stairs (not on display) are entered from the Nursery Corridor, where they conveniently access the Kitchen and Servants' Hall on the ground floor, Nursery on the first floor, and female staff accommodation at the top of the house. While the female stairs are made of wood, presumably for their lighter frames, the men's cantilever staircase is made of stone. This steep staircase links the Butler's Rooms, Kitchen, Lamp Room, Servants' Hall and Luggage Lift on the ground floor, the first-floor bedrooms and, at the top of the house, the luggage storage and male accommodation. Both staircases adjoin the Servants' Hall, where male and female staff met on common ground. The colour scheme of blue and terracotta with red oxide skirting boards is based on the original, mimicking those in the Kitchen Quarters.

The Sluice Room

Close to the male and female staff stairs is the Sluice Room, which provided all the housekeeping needs for the first-floor rooms. Domestic equipment was stored here; coal would be distributed; removed ashes dealt with; and the chamber-maids would pour slops down the sluice under the windows. The *luggage lift* outside carried coal, stores and equipment.

Ascend the stairs past the top of the luggage lift. Ahead is the Linen Lobby.

At the top of the Stone Stairs is an early 19th-century, eight-day, striking, *longcase clock* made by John Broad of Bodmin.

(Right) The Linen Room

The Linen Room

The house linen was stored in this room, which also separated the male and female staff accommodation. The colour of these cupboards and the bedroom doors was known as 'Housekeeper's Drab'. The door leading from the back of the room adjoins a corridor leading to three female staff bedrooms and a drying room (not on display).

Before the fire, there was a laundry in the house. Afterwards, the family sent washing to the charitable foundations of the House of Mercy in Bodmin and St Faith's Home for Fallen Women at Lostwithiel. The latter was built by the architect G. E. Street on land given by Lord Robartes.

The Male Staff Bedrooms

The family recruited staff from Cornwall and London. Being a benevolent family, they gave opportunities to underprivileged children to work in service, which at least gave them a roof over their heads and food on their plates. The bedrooms are simply laid out and provided a private space in which to relax.

The Footmen's Livery Room

These wardrobes once housed the liveries of the male staff. During the late 19th century, when the household was significantly smaller, the Agar-Robartes sisters used the built-in wardrobes to store their dresses. Today, the livery of the Tregoning family of Landue near Launceston is on display. These three livery suits were made in 1904 at a cost of £68 for the servants of John Tregoning, High Sheriff of Cornwall.

Nowhere is the separation between family and staff so obvious. The fine plasterwork and sumptuous panelling encountered on the Teak Bedroom Staircase landing contrasts strikingly with the staff quarters: even the door leading on to the stairs has a high- and low-status side. Straight across the landing are more attic bedrooms (not on display) that were used for additional staff accommodation.

(Left) A servant's bedroom   (Below) The Luggage Room

As the family grew, so did the staff. In 1851 only three members of staff were resident in the house. By 1881 this figure had risen to eleven, seven of those being female. Most of the staff would have travelled to the family's London homes during the summer season, which left only a skeleton staff here.

On the bed in the first bedroom is a yellow and black waistcoat from the early 20th-century livery of the Agar-Robartes family.

The Luggage Room

Cut deep into the attics, this dark and musty room is redolent of the railway age, when the smallest country station had porters to heave the dome-topped trunks and heavy leather portmanteaux.

The Teak Bedroom Staircase

In the alcove is a burr-walnut, mid-18th-century *longcase clock* made by Ferdinand Vigne of London.

Pictures

In descending order, *Ponti del Pasana* by Myles Birket Foster RWS (1825–99), *Figures in the Street* by Peter De Wint (1784–1849), two unidentified girls after Jean-Baptiste Greuze (1725–1805), and *Beauvais Cathedral and Market* by Alfred Montague, 1864. High on the wall is a full-length portrait of *The Agar-Robartes Children* by Anna Lea Merritt, 1885. Her evocative portrayal of the elder children of the 2nd Lord Robartes shows the five-years-old twins Tommy (in black) and Everilda, Gerald as a baby in a blue frock and the eldest, Mary Vere. At the foot of the stairs is a delightful portrait by Henry Weigall (1829–1925) of *The Hon. Cecil Agar-Robartes.*

On the first-floor landing are two fine portraits by the accomplished portrait and figurative painter Richard Jack RA (1866–1952). First, *The Hon. Violet Agar-Robartes (1888–1965)*, dated 1914 and second, between the ground and first floors, *The Hon. Thomas (Tommy) Agar-Robartes MP (1880–1915)* dated 1907. Violet was the third daughter of the 6th Viscount Clifden. Tommy was held in such high esteem by the Cornish electorate that despite being disqualified from his seat in 1906 for 'irregularities', 15,000 Cornish Liberals subscribed to this portrait. Tommy is shown here presenting the first reading of the Land Tenure Bill in the House of Commons. He was widely regarded as a dandy and 'the best dressed man in Parliament', always wearing a bunch of violets in his lapel. Alongside is a half-length portrait of him whilst at Eton by J. Hanson Walker (1844–1933).

Further down the staircase is another portrait by Hanson Walker of *The Hon. Gerald Agar-Robartes (1883–1966)*. The full-length portrait beside it was painted by James Sant RA (1820–1916) and shows the *Hon. Victor and the Hon. Violet Agar-Robartes.*

On the wall to the right of the Corner Room door is a portrait of *Dolly Pentreath of Mousehole (1685–1777)*, who was reputedly the last person just to speak Cornish.

Please feel free to use the Corner Room to rest. Follow the corridor to your left passing the corridor portraits and then left again.

The Corridor

Pictures

A list of pictures compiled soon after the fire of 1881 shows that very few family portraits were destroyed. However, Old Master paintings by Ludovico Carracci, Luca Giordano, François Le Moyne and Filippo Lauri were not so fortunate. This collection of family portraits was listed in an 1845 inventory and was bequeathed by the 7th Viscount Clifden to the National Trust.

The two oval portraits show the owner of Lanhydrock from 1758, *George Hunt MP (c.1720–98)*, and *The Hon. Henry Booth (1687–1726)*, who was related through his grandmother's family. On the wall opposite are *John Hunt of Mollington (1684–1739)* and his wife *Dorcas Amphlett*. The Hunt family married into the Robartes family in 1719. On the end wall are two portraits which have recently been identified as *Col Thomas Hunt MP (1599–1669)* and his wife *Elizabeth Owen*. This staunchly Puritan couple were great-great-grandparents to George Hunt of Lanhydrock. Alongside is *Henry Robartes, 3rd Earl of Radnor (c.1695–1741)* and opposite is *Lady Rachel Russell, Countess of Bridgwater* by Charles Jervas (c.1675–1739).

Turn left into His Lordship's Corridor, where there are numerous late Victorian watercolours of Cornish scenes. The second door on the left leads to His Lordship's Bedroom.

(Right) Thomas, Everilda, Gerald and Mary Agar-Robartes; by Anna Lea Merritt, 1885 (Teak Bedroom Staircase)

His Lordship's Bedroom

Lord Robartes chose this modest room as his bedroom, although the architect originally intended to give him a much grander room. The *bed* is a single half-tester of *c*.1860, whilst the *wallpaper* is a copy of that designed by A.W.N. Pugin for the Robing Room of the House of Lords. The 1886 inventory shows that only two bathrooms were installed in the post-fire house, so it is not surprising to find several saucer baths amongst the contents.

Pass through the Bathroom and then into Her Ladyship's Bedroom.

The Bathroom

Originally intended as a dressing room for his Lordship, this room contains two peculiar door arrangements. First, the door-frame leading from His Lordship's Bedroom towards Her Ladyship's is unusually small. The 2nd Lord Robartes was 5 ft 4 in tall and was affectionately known as 'Little Lordy' – the door presumably made him appear bigger than he really was. Second, a double-door arrangement connects it to Her Ladyship's Bedroom. It would not have been considered impolite for Her Ladyship to lock her own bedroom door to ensure privacy.

Her Ladyship's Bedroom

This room has an impressive barrel-vaulted ceiling and an overmantel, which, although Victorian, celebrates the marriage of John Robartes and his second wife Letitia in 1646/7. It was often the case in large houses that the lady's bedroom did not have an associated dressing room; rather, the maids would bring washing facilities into the room, when required.

The dressing-table is heavily draped with lace in the fashion of the day. Beside the dressing-table is a secure night safe for her Ladyship's jewels. The Meissen porcelain was a wedding present in 1878.

The dressing-table in Her Ladyship's Bedroom

Pictures

The picture by the door is of *Thomas Charles Agar-Robartes* painted by his mother Juliana. She was a talented amateur artist, taught by the Plymouth painter Nicholas Condy. Above this is a charming sketch of *Thomas James Agar-Robartes* painted by C.B.E. Bowden in 1840. The two drawings dated 1879 by George Richmond to the right of the west door depict Lady Robartes's parents *F.H. and Caroline Dickinson of Kingweston*. A fine Pre-Raphaelite-style painting of *The Madonna with Attendant Angels* by John Melhuish Strudwick (1849–1937) is near the doorway through to the Boudoir.

The Boudoir

This very feminine room adjoins the Drawing Room and Her Ladyship's Bedroom, allowing an easy ebb and flow of public reception and private retirement. The plasterwork *overmantel* seems to represent the story of the *Judgement of Paris*, although the representations of the

(Left) His Lordship's Bedroom   (Right) The Boudoir

central characters appear jumbled. Perhaps the Victorian builders were attempting to re-create one of the pre-fire overmantels from memory.

Furnishings

In the window is an alabaster, eight-day striking, French *mantel-clock* with ormolu mounts made *c.*1860. On the far side of the room is a 19th-century *automaton*. Made by Gustav Vichy of Paris, the mechanical Jumeau doll plays the piano when wound. The silver *tea service* was made by A.B. Savory & Sons of London in 1882–3. The silver-plated *muffin warmer* dates from 1877. In the small display case are several pieces of oriental *filigree silver* collected by Alexander Agar-Robartes, when he was ADC to the Viceroy of India in the early 1920s.

Pictures

The four drawings dated 1881 and 1884 by William Edward Miller (active 1873–1903) show the four eldest Agar-Robartes children, Mary Vere, Thomas, Everilda and Gerald. On the south wall are two further paintings dated 1896 by Augusto Stoppoloni (1855–1910) of *The Hon. Violet Agar-Robartes* and *The Hon. Cecil Agar-Robartes*.

The Drawing Room (south end)

This room was entered from the double doors at the top of the Oak Stairs. Before the fire, it was two separate rooms – a drawing room to the north (far end), known as the Cedar Room, and a cedar bedroom to the south. The small alcove over the entrance porch still retains its pre-fire cedarwood panelling. During the late 19th century, the Agar-Robartes family filled this room with furniture in order to create informal spaces. Here they could relax, read and write letters.

Ceramics and furniture

On display are many pieces of Chinese *famille verte porcelain* dating from *c.*1690 to 1720. The 18th-century set of English, giltwood *chairs and walnut-framed sofas and settees* was brought to Lanhydrock from Wimpole Hall in the 1930s. They were re-upholstered for a visit by Queen Victoria to Wimpole in 1844. Queen Victoria made an unplanned visit to Lanhydrock in September 1846 – unfortunately, the family were out! Also on display are a pair of side-tables, *c.*1750, and an English walnut writing-desk, *c.*1720.

Pictures

The general arrangement here follows that of the 1880s. On the chimneypiece wall are portraits of *Lady Mary Booth (d.1741),* wife of Russell Robartes and pictured with her son *Henry* and sister *Lady Lucy Booth (1646/9–1723).* Both ladies were daughters of the 1st Earl of Warrington of Dunham Massey in Cheshire. Henry became 3rd Earl of Radnor after his uncle, Charles Bodville Robartes MP, died

Thomas, 6th Viscount Clifden with his wife Mary and two of their children in the Drawing Room, c.1905

without a son. Either side of the Vauxhall plate pier-glass in an enamel and gilt frame, *c.*1710, are *Charles Bodville Robartes, 2nd Earl of Radnor (1660–1723)*, pictured on the south wall alongside his wife *Elizabeth Cutler (d.1697)*. These portraits were painted by Michael Dahl (1656/7–1743) and Sir Godfrey Kneller (1646/9–1723) respectively. Elizabeth Cutler was heiress to Sir John Cutler, a wealthy London merchant famous for his private miserliness and public generosity. Her marriage (apparently without approval) in 1689 brought with it Wimpole Hall, where together they laid out outstanding gardens and completed extensive work on the interiors. However, such extravagance soon caught up with him, and after his wife's death Robartes sold the Wimpole estate.

In the small Alcove Room is a portrait of *Soame Jenyns MP (1704–87)* after Sir Joshua Reynolds. This is the only inventoried painting from the London home of Anna Maria Hunt's mother, Mary (1740–1824), still in the collection.

The Nativity; by Evelyn de Morgan (Prayer Room)

Leave from the same door and turn right into the corridor. The first room on the left is the Prayer Room.

The Prayer Room

In the late 18th century a private Prayer Room was created here from the upper part of a 17th-century chapel. The ritual of family prayers was common in the strong religious climate of most Victorian households. The devout Robartes family would have prayed here every morning during the week; on Sunday there were regular services in the nearby church.

After the fire, this room was refurbished using cedar panelling salvaged from the pre-fire Drawing Room. The impressive Rococo-style Bath stone *fireplace* was designed by James

MacLaren. The passenger lift substantially reduces the size of this room. Although planned in 1882, it was not installed until 1928, presumably for the ailing 2nd Lord Robartes.

Pictures

On the wall are *St Luke writing his Gospel at the Dictation of the Virgin Mary* by Clement O. Skilbeck (1865–1954) and a chalk and charcoal drawing entitled *The Nativity*, signed 'EP' for Evelyn Pickering (later De Morgan). The two framed prints, *Suffer Little Children* and *The Nativity*, were given by Lady Robartes to her young sons Tommy and Gerald in 1889.

Pass the top of the Oak Stairs on your left, and view the Drawing Room through the double doors on your right. Pass through into the Morning Room.

The Morning Room

Used as a room in which to read the daily papers or just while away the time after breakfast, morning rooms were common in most large Victorian houses. Ideally, the room should be east-facing in order to catch the early sun. This room, however, faces north. It adjoins the Drawing Room, and sliding doors enabled you to extend the space, if required. When the Victorian family performed plays in the room, the sliding doors acted as the stage curtain.

The *overmantel* is a survival from the 17th century and celebrates the second marriage of John Robartes, 2nd Baron, and the young Letitia Smith. The motto *Quae Supra* is taken from St Paul's warning: 'Set your affection on things above, not on things on earth' (*Colossians*, iii, 2).

Tapestries

The two 17th-century tapestries were hung soon after the refurbishment was completed in 1885. At the time they were valued at £150. The first, *A Peasant Scene*, is Flemish after David Teniers the Younger (1610–90), woven by Pierre (1712–63) and François (1720–75) van der Borcht. The second is an English Mortlake tapestry showing *A Fountain (May)* from a set that depicted the months of the year.

Furniture and ceramics

The two French tortoiseshell and gilded brass *writing-tables* date from the early 18th century, as do the two Dutch mahogany inlaid *display cases*. In the display cabinets is a collection of mid-18th-century soft-paste porcelain. In the room itself are a garniture of Chinese *famille verte* porcelain (*c.*1690–1720) and a collection of Chinese blue-and-white porcelain vases dating from the 17th to the 19th centuries.

Pass through into the Drawing Room (north end).

The Drawing Room (north end)

The family often held musical recitals, with each of the children performing in turn, accompanied by the piano. By the window is an early Victorian *piano* by John Broadwood.

Furnishings

On the floor is a rare English mid-19th-century wool chenille *carpet*. The English *chandeliers* with French crystals were made for gas, but converted to electricity before they were installed in 1896. A fine collection of late 18th-century *Worcester porcelain* decorated with a dragon pattern is housed in the mahogany china cabinet. The furniture, along with the plants and screens, made effective room dividers, ensuring some seclusion in a busy Victorian household.

Pictures

On the west wall, either side of the sliding doors to the Morning Room, are portraits of mother and daughter, Mrs Mary Hunt and Anna Maria Hunt. The Lancashire heiress *Mary Hunt (1740–1824)* was painted by Joseph Wright of

(Right) The Morning Room

(Above) The Drawing Room looking south

Derby soon after her marriage to Thomas Hunt of Mollington Hall in 1765. Wright, better known for his depictions of the Industrial Revolution, worked as a portraitist in Liverpool between 1768 and 1771. His works from this period reflected and helped to define taste in the growing mercantile city. Mary Hunt lived in South Audley Street, London, and from 1804 her newly married daughter lived in the adjoining house at 1 Dean Street. *Anna Maria Hunt (1771–1861)* was painted by George Romney (1734–1802) in seven sittings between 30 March and 1 June 1792 at his studio in Cavendish Square, London. The dog was added later. Anna Maria was a very affectionate and considerate daughter. Both ladies were regular visitors to Lanhydrock and were constant companions, spending summer seasons in Brighton, Tunbridge Wells and Ramsgate, as well as making excursions to the family home of Bold Hall in Lancashire.

On the east wall opposite is a portrait of the Welsh heiress *Sarah Bodville, The Hon. Mrs Robert Robartes (d.1720)* after Sir Peter Lely. She was the mother of the 2nd Earl of Radnor and was considered a 'great beauty, and a fine lady indeed' by Samuel Pepys. On her marriage to Robert Robartes in 1657, she brought an estate worth £30,000. Above the radiator is a portrait of *Mary Langham, Countess of Warrington (d.1690)* by Sir Peter Lely and studio. Her daughter, Mary, married Russell Robartes in 1694. The Warrington family home was Dunham Massey in Cheshire, and this black and gold livery frame is typical of the Warrington collection.

Furniture

A Victorian walnut circular inlaid *centre-table* carries a display of Royal photographs. The three continental marquetry *commodes* date from *c.*1750–1800. A collection of 18th-century blue-john mounted *urns* sits on the mantelpiece. Blue-john is a rare mineral found near Castleton in Derbyshire.

Pass through into the Gallery.

The Gallery

This long chamber survived the fire and was originally one of two galleries in the house. Multiple galleries were common in large 17th-century houses; indeed, the more galleries on show, the more impressive the building. This room initially served as a garden chamber, looking north over the extensive planned landscape. At the far end of the room was a doorway that led into another gallery that looked eastwards over the deer-park. The whole east range, including its gallery, was demolished about 1784.

The granite *fireplaces* are of a style and with markings quite common in Cornwall. They appear to have been salvaged from an earlier house or perhaps, as John Loveday wrote in 1736, 'Part of the [Restormel Castle] Stone was carried off years ago to build at Llanhidrock above one mile off'. The high-level carved *frieze*, original painted *plasterwork panelling* (concealed behind the radiator grilles) and decorated *window panels* are further features that survive from the original house.

The Gallery was used to display family portraits, as a place to exercise during inclement weather, and during the early 19th century as a library with a billiard-table. The High Victorian family used the space as a large reception room, albeit separated into smaller informal spaces complete with writing-desks, family portraits, a Broadwood piano and other fine furniture and ornament. The 7th Viscount Clifden amassed a very important collection of furniture that was disposed of at auctions during the 1950s and 1960s. The National Trust has deliberately thinned out the room and given

How was the ceiling made?

The ceiling is constructed of oak lathes suspended across the rafters and purlins to create the barrel formwork within the 'A' frame. A prepared mixture of slaked lime would have been mixed with sand and fine hair or straw and then applied to the lathes. The ceiling would then be ready to receive the ribwork, with moulds filled with wet plaster pressed into it. The more complex designs were made on the ground, mitred and worked up with lime putty. Plaster-coated iron pendants were installed both as lighting fixings and to conceal the more difficult mitres. At some point, the ceiling became structurally unsound. Consequently, hundreds of ropes or wires were tied through the ceiling and secured to the timberwork above.

Noah's Ark; a panel from the Gallery plasterwork ceiling

The Gallery about 1890

it a more formal appearance so that the books, pictures and architectural features create the main focus.

Plasterwork

The 35-metre-long barrel-vaulted ceiling is a masterpiece of the plasterer's art. While the design cannot be attributed to any specific craftsman or date, it does belong to the tradition of south-west plasterwork that developed over several decades in the late 16th and early 17th centuries. Other examples are or were evident at nearby Prideaux Place (*c.*1593) and Trewan (1633–5), and as far afield as Dunsland (1610) in Devon and Sherborne Castle (1630) in Dorset.

The 24 cartouches or panels on the ceiling depict episodes from the Old Testament Book of Genesis. The narrative sequence starts at the far, east, end of the Gallery, which would have

originally been the main entrance. The animals were copied from illustrations in volumes by Conrad Gessner (1551–8) and Edward Topsell (1607).

The lunette above the door and the two fireplace overmantels were based on engravings by Ambrosius Francken, which were published in Gerald de Iode's *Thesaurus* (1585): *David slaying Goliath, Saul throwing the javelin at David* and *David taking the pitcher and spear from Saul's tent.* The choice of these particular episodes from the Book of Samuel represents a statement of family support for the anointed king, but whether this was Richard Robartes's allegiance to James I or John Robartes's to Charles I, we cannot be certain. The plasterwork achievement in the lunette at the opposite end of the room celebrates the marriage of John Robartes, later 1st Earl of Radnor, to Lucy Rich in 1630, which provides a date for this part of the plasterwork.

Books

The historic core of the Lanhydrock library was created between 1590 and 1685, making it the earliest large collection of books in the care of the National Trust. It includes no fewer than 25 incunables (books printed before 1501) and such extreme rarities as a unique copy of the earliest known English ABC, which was printed in London about 1535.

The library was the work of four men – Thomas Peter, Hannibal Gamon, Walter Snell and John Robartes – through whose hands it passed in succession. Peter was a native of Devon who was educated at Oxford, where he seems to have begun buying books in the 1590s. He was appointed Rector of nearby St Mawgan in 1603. After his death in 1618, Peter was succeeded as Rector by Hannibal Gamon, who married his widow Elizabeth and inherited his books. Before his appointment, Gamon had also studied at Oxford, where he had assembled a scholarly library strong in theology, church

history, law and the Latin Classics. The copious annotations in Gamon's books reveal him to have been a learned and moderate Anglican (and not a Puritan, as has often been asserted). Nor is there any evidence that he served as the Robartes family chaplain, although he was certainly held in high esteem by the family, being asked to preach at Frances Robartes's funeral in 1627. On Gamon's death in 1651, the by-now substantial library seems to have passed to Walter Snell (who was the chaplain at Lanhydrock) and via him to John Robartes. Robartes, who was also educated at Oxford, added works on theology, history, politics and science to the library. Like Gamon, he annotated his books, with comments both serious and flippant.

With Robartes's death in 1685, active collecting seems to have ceased. Despite 18th-century neglect, removal to the Gallery and some heavy-handed rebinding in the 19th

The Lanhydrock Atlas of 1694–7

The four volumes of the Lanhydrock Atlas comprise 258 beautifully executed water-colour-on-vellum maps, each measuring 51 × 40.6 cm. Commissioned by the 2nd Earl of Radnor, the vibrantly coloured maps are unsigned, but have been attributed to the eminent 17th-century cartographer Joel Gascoyne. Because they were working documents in constant use, they had to be rebound in leather in the 19th century.

As a collection, the maps are significant for several reasons. First, they document approx-imately 50,000 acres of Cornwall owned at the end of the 17th century by the Earl of Radnor.

Second, they contain a manorial survey, care-fully detailing acreage of plots and definition of boundaries, while also recording buildings, roads, tenements and, sometimes, names of tenants. Third, they define land use: pasture, arable, meadow, common ground and woods.

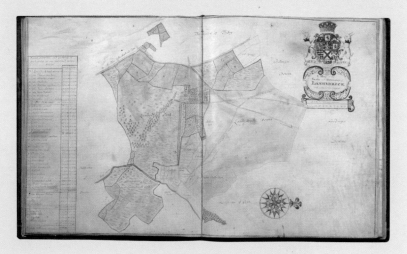

(Above) *The Gallery today*

century, the 1881 fire and discreet sales in the early 20th century, the bulk of the historic library survived to be inherited by the National Trust with the house. Today, it is once again appreciated as Lanhydrock's outstanding treasure.

Pictures

To the right of the stairs is a reduced copy of *Elizabeth Cutler, Countess of Radnor (d. 1697)* by Sir Godfrey Kneller, while to the left is a likely portrait of her father, *Sir John Cutler*.

On the north wall facing the gardens are *Mr and Mrs Thomas Hunt II* by Sir Godfrey Kneller. At the end of the Gallery is a portrait of *Thomas Hunt III of Mollington MP (1721–88)* by

the West-Country painter Thomas Hudson. Alongside is a fine portrait by George Romney of *Mary Bold, Mrs Thomas Hunt (1740–1824)*, mother of Anna Maria.

On the opposite south (fireplace) wall is a portrait of *Mary, Duchess of Chandos* by the school of John Riley. Alongside the window are portraits of *Thomas Hunt II* attributed to Michael Dahl and of *Henry, 3rd Earl of Radnor*. Above the bookpress are *George Hunt MP (1720?–98)* and *Mary Lloyd, Lady Mainwaring*, both by Jervas. To the left of the fireplace are two portraits by Thomas Hudson of *Elizabeth* and *Frances Hunt*, daughters of Thomas and Mary Vere Hunt. To the right of the fireplace is *George Hunt MP* in his uniform as an officer in the Cheshire Yeomanry.

Furniture

They are predominately family pieces. Along the north wall (looking towards the garden) are an 18th-century Chinese black-lacquered *cabinet* decorated with birds and foliage and a late 17th-century walnut *cabinet* on spiral turned legs flanked by a pair of Charles II walnut *elbow chairs*. Along the south wall are a Flemish ebony and red tortoiseshell veneered *cabinet* of *c.*1680; a William and Mary walnut and feather banded *writing-desk*; two mid-17th-century *elbow chairs* with eagle crestings; and a walnut-framed *settee* on cabriole legs with an unusual turned stretcher. This settee was transferred to Lanhydrock after the sale of Wimpole Hall. Throughout the room is a set of late 18th-century mahogany *side-chairs* with canvas-work embroidered covers. These chairs appear in the two Lanhydrock inventories of 1799.

On the radiator covers are three 19th-century plaster copies of *busts* of the Roman emperors Nero and Caracalla, and Medea, the mythical priestess of ancient Greece. The *orrery* or planetarium on the centre-table once belonged to Lady Mendip, great-aunt of the 1st Lord Robartes. This 18th-century scientific instrument displays the movement of planets around the sun.

Retrace your steps through the Morning Room and on to the Oak Staircase.

The Oak Staircase

This grand staircase serves the first-floor reception rooms. Much of the staircase was salvaged from the fire of 1881, although its original date remains unclear. At the half-landing there was a convenient passage from the house to the family pew in the parish church.

Pictures

On the landing and stairs both wives of John Robartes (1606–85), later 1st Earl of Radnor, can be seen. John himself, from the studio of Godfrey Kneller, is pictured in his robes as Lord Privy Seal alongside a portrait of his first wife *Lucy Rich (c.1615/6–before 1646/7)* in the style of

Sir Peter Lely. Lucy was raised at Leez Priory in Essex, the home of the Earl of Warwick, a Parliamentarian of deep religious belief and strong political fervour. Her marriage to the like-minded Robartes was perhaps therefore seen as an ideal union. Yet her time at Lanhydrock was fraught with 'many sorrows', which included the Royalist seizure of the Lanhydrock estate and imprisonment of her children. When Lucy died, Robartes married her cousin, *Letitia Smith (c.1630–1714)*, pictured on the landing by Sir Peter Lely. During the first fifteen years of their marriage she bore him fourteen children. Charles II restored Robartes to favour after 1660, and the family moved to Danvers House in Chelsea, which Pepys called 'the prettiest contrived house that I ever saw in my life'. Letitia's striking beauty and benevolent piety made her an instant court favourite; one commentator even suggested that she had had an affair with the future James II.

Descend the stairs.

High on the staircase wall is a large English school portrait of *Sir Richard Robartes (c.1580–1634)*. On the ground floor is a mid-17th-century portrait of *Robert Robartes, Viscount Bodmin MP (1633–82)*. Robert was eldest son of the 1st Earl of Radnor.

The Music Room and Stone Hall (Shop)

The fine plasterwork ceiling dates from the late 17th century and shows a distinct progression from Jacobean to Restoration architectural fashions. Once the Great Dining Room and later a ballroom, after the fire this room was designated by the architect as the Library. Although interior designs were drawn up for a new Library, the books remained in the Gallery. By the early 19th century a large pipe-organ was installed across the corner of the room. The next room, the Stone Hall, was the original entrance to the pre-*c.*1621 manor house. The flagstones are original, and stairs once led down to a wine cellar.

The Service Courtyard and Church

The Coach House and Harness Block

The Jacobean stables were first considered for replacement in the middle of the 19th century. The 1st Lord Robartes, who was said to be 'very particular about his horses', commissioned plans for new stables and outbuildings, first from a Bodmin architect, Joseph Pascoe, in the Classical style, and second from the London-based Gothicist George Truefitt (1824–1902). Neither design was executed. Instead, a new Coach House was built in 1857, when the eminent Victorian architect George Gilbert Scott was commissioned to carry out essential repairs in the house. This building in the modern Gothic style provided space for the three carriages in the central portion with stables either side, each containing three boxes for both heavy carriage horses and ponies. The stable was subdivided in the 1890s to house the Shetland ponies and three dogs belonging to the Agar-Robartes children. Above is a gallery leading towards the hayloft, where hay or chaff would have been stored. The hay was pitched into the loft through the exterior doors in the upper storey. To ensure effective timekeeping by the staff, an eight-day turret clock with dead-beat escapement was installed in 1906.

The Harness Block provided further stabling for five riding horses on the ground floor, with living accommodation for the grooms above. The original Jacobean building was demolished soon after the fire, and more modern facilities supplied by Coad in a style similar to that of the extended house. Towards the end of the 19th century an E-shaped Kennels building was erected about 500m north-east of the house. Today this building is used as office space.

The Church

St Hydroc's Church continues to thrive at the heart of the Lanhydrock parish, holding services every Sunday, details of which can be found in the church porch. The National Trust does not own the church, but does help in its upkeep. The church welcomes donations.

The church was built in the mid-15th century, but may incorporate an earlier church or chapel. Lanhydrock means the site of somebody called Hydroc. Since 1478, when William Worcester visited the Augustinian Priory of St Petroc in Bodmin, the little understood *Sanctus Ydroc* (St Hydroc) has been regarded as the church's patron saint. Until the Dissolution of the Monasteries in 1539, the church was dependent on the priory and served a small community.

Situated to the rear of the house, the church now consists of a porch, nave, chancel, two side-aisles (probably added *c.*1620) and a three-stage tower. The Robartes family crypt lies beneath the old family pews, which were positioned 'At the east end of the south side … on which are carved the arms of Sir Richard Robartes, bart. and those of Frances Hender, his lady'. In 1626 Frances was the first member of the family to be interred here. This committal space was not exclusive to the Robartes family; indeed, members of the Carminow family, as well as the Robarteses' family chaplain, Walter Snell, and two loyal servants, rest here. The last was Henry Robartes, 3rd Earl of Radnor, whose body was brought back from Paris in 1741.

The diary of Philippa and Edith Dickinson records a visit to Lanhydrock church on Sunday, 19 October 1879: 'Very wet this morning. Service at 11. Lord and Lady R, M & T [Mary Dickinson and Thomas Charles Agar-Robartes] sat in the square pew & the rest in another. Whole thing very old fashioned indeed. Afternoon still wet. Church at 3. In the evening we sang some songs.' A week later the same, but 'Dee & I went up to see the Sunday school at the Gate House'.

By 1745 the parish was considered 'one of the least in the Diocese', relying 'entirely upon the generosity of the family of Lanhydrock'. With Anna Maria Agar's tenure of the estate its fortunes revived. In 1808 the aptly named Mr Chapple provided an estimate for alterations amounting to £384 18s 4d. At this time the oak pews were removed and replaced with pine. The focus of worship was the pulpit, which was positioned against the north wall under the fine 1621 plasterwork panel depicting the arms of James I and beside the funeral hatchment of Charles Agar (d. 1811). In 1824 F. W. L. Stockdale described the church as a 'beautiful small edifice, with an embattled tower, finely mantled with ivy. It has recently undergone a complete repair … judiciously preserved as much as possible.' In 1844 a regular parish was created at Lord Robartes's expense.

Between 1886 and 1888 George Vialls of Ealing, London, carried out a full restoration, paid for by the Agar-Robartes family in memory of Thomas James and Juliana Agar-Robartes.

The main alteration was to focus the centre of worship towards the chancel (rather than the pulpit on the north wall), which was extended to allow more room in the Sacrarium. Vialls also introduced a modern variegated–marble mosaic pavement in the nave (installed by Burke & Co. of London and Paris), a carved white alabaster reredos, depicting *The Last Supper,* by Earp & Hobbs of London, and a new east window by Clayton & Bell, which was paid for by the estate tenants. This fine stained glass depicts the Ascension, the Crucifixion, the Baptism of the Lord, the Nativity, the Agony in the Garden and the Burial. The granite and serpentine font was a gift of Lord and Lady Robartes and is inscribed in memory of their son John Radnor, who died aged only six months. John Radnor was interred in the new family vault in the churchyard, which contains three generations of the Agar-Robartes family. After the First World War a new window was inserted in memory of Tommy Agar-Robartes, who perished at the Battle of Loos in 1915.

The Church

The Garden

The earliest depiction of the gardens appears in the Lanhydrock Atlas of 1694–7. Included in the 22-acre 17th-century layout were a flower garden, a pheasantry, kitchen garden, pear garden and orchard, and a bowling green to the north, with a wilderness garden beyond. Far from being wild or unkempt, the wilderness was a carefully planned and maintained part of the landscape with biblical connotations of Adam and Eve's banishment into the uncultivated wilderness and Christ's retreat into the wilderness. Perhaps in this context the garden became a living illustration of the Gallery plasterwork. A letter of 1803 still referred to the 'Wilderness near the North Gate'.

As the house fell into decline, so the garden followed. By the early 19th century any surviving formal garden arrangement had been swept away, being replaced by a more picturesque and natural outlook, with the parklands flowing up to the house. This kind of landscape was advocated by Humphry Repton (1752–1818), who influenced Cornish gardens through his work at Antony House, Caerhays Castle, Port Eliot, Tregothnan and Trewarthenick. One benefit of this style was that the redundant Gatehouse became a fashionable landscape folly.

Trends in gardening rarely remain static, and by the middle of the 19th century the fashion for the Italian garden was gaining popularity. In 1854 the fledgling architect George Truefitt (1824–1902), based in Bloomsbury Square, London, was commissioned to prepare a garden plan. Truefitt proposed a geometric layout with water features, terracing, gravelled walkways and a promenade walk. He also envisaged that the Gatehouse would form the central focus to the eastern vista down the 17th-century avenue. The garden would be enclosed by a wall to the north and east, and new outbuildings to the south. The gardens that were eventually laid out by Coad in 1858 were based on Truefitt's designs, but Coad added features of his own,

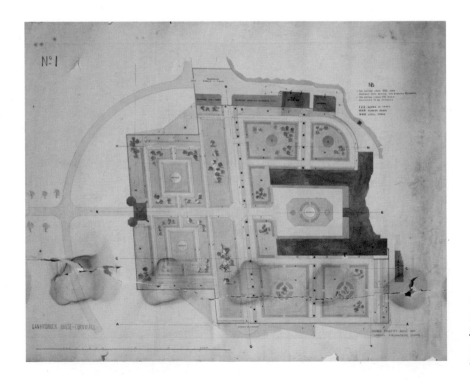

George Truefitt's 1854 design for the formal gardens, on which Richard Coad's final plan was based

such as the granite flight of steps to the church with a seat beneath that was later the favourite sitting place of the 7th Viscount Clifden.

Neither Truefitt nor Coad made any reference to planting – presumably because this was not part of their brief. It is likely that Juliana Agar-Robartes, who had a particular interest in gardening, and her head gardener, Joseph Bray, decided the planting. Photographs from *c.*1860 show the 29 sentinel yews – the Irish 'Florence Court' variety (*Taxus baccata* 'Fastigiata') – alongside a curious mixture of exotic plants, shrubs, herbaceous perennials, geraniums and monkey puzzle trees. To the north were, as now, boxed-edged geometric beds, although then the pathways were raked with gravel dividing the beds, whilst now they are grass.

The family had a talent for planting wisely, building on the success of their predecessors. During the 20th century Gerald, 7th Viscount Clifden, who was a very keen gardener, introduced the fine collection of camellias, rhododendrons and Himalayan magnolias. He also acquired the impressive bronze urns that had once been part of Lord Hertford's collection at the château de Bagatelle near Paris. These 17th-century urns, modelled by Louis Ballin, goldsmith to Louis XIV, were at Nether Swell, Gloucestershire, before coming to Cornwall. Further changes in the 20th century included the loss of the gravelled walkways and the relocation of some of the steps.

Just outside the formal gardens were once a croquet lawn and a tennis court. By the north wall are two large copper beech trees planted by W. E. Gladstone in 1889 and in 1905 by his fellow Liberal Lord Rosebery. To the west are the higher gardens, which offer spectacular views across the estate. These gardens were originally laid out in the 1860s, but by 1930 they were described as having 'nothing but Portugal laurel'. A herbaceous half-circle was laid out in 1914, while further additions were added in 1915 from plans made by W. Goldring of the Royal Horticultural Society.

The Parterre today

In more recent years the 28 acres of gardens have been exceptionally maintained by a succession of long-serving head gardeners including George Potter, Peter Borlase BEM and Nigel Teagle. Successive garden teams have ensured Lanhydrock's position as one of the finest gardens in the South-West.

The Kitchen Garden

The Kitchen Garden was once in what we today refer to as the High Garden. The part-cob-constructed Thatched House with a later stone façade was probably once occupied by the kitchen gardener. Its position, near the main water source, would make this a good location. However, in 1840 plans were drawn up for a new Kitchen Garden situated to the south of the house, overlooking the Fowey valley. The plan shows that within the garden was a melonry, with an independent boiler, a couple of orchards as well as beds for the cultivation of seakale, raspberries, rhubarb and asparagus. Garden Cottage, positioned at the front of the Kitchen Garden, was refurbished as a single house with new grand ironwork installed where the Agar-Robartes family passed through to visit the gardens. The simple porch was added for the family to enter in order to discuss matters with the Head Gardener in the relative comfort of his Best Parlour. Today, this walled garden is used to propagate plants for many National Trust properties in the South-West.

The Parkland

'The beauties of the surrounding country add the final charm to one of the most picturesque houses in Cornwall.'

Country Life, 1903

The precision of the formal garden contrasts with the apparently natural parkland. The wider landscape has always added an important aesthetic value to the house. Indeed, several generations have deliberately planted to enhance the extensive views towards the Fowey valley. About 1648 John, 2nd Baron Robartes planted a single avenue of sycamore aligned with the front of the house in order to create a spectacular approach. (It may also have been intended to celebrate the victory of the Parliamentary army in the English Civil War.) To the south of the avenue was once the largest deer-park in Cornwall, enclosing 259 acres from Greatwood down to the flood plain of the River Fowey at Higginsmoor and then rising steeply across the river to Bromquin Wood (now Brownqueen). This flood plain is now interlaced by a network of streams and pools – a legacy of the streaming works carried out by tin miners during the 16th century. Remnants of the old deer-wall can still be seen on the estate, with the best section in the Maudlin valley.

In 1758 William Borlase reported that the park contained a 'great variety of up and down Wood, some fine and scattered … but the Spine is cold. Black and ferny and the chief vista comes too near in all reason to the house and

crowds it.' The deer herd was given up soon after 1758 during the tenure of George Hunt. In the early 19th century more radical changes were made by his niece, Anna Maria Hunt. She added an outer row of beech to the single sycamore avenue, planted a clump of trees known as the Round on the slope to the south-east of the house, and created ornamental drives, an arboretum and new plantations. In 1821 the steward wrote: 'The plantations at Lanhydrock were completed last winter and the trees now look remarkably well – in 10–20 years they will be a beautiful ornament to the place.' A year later 10,000 large forest trees were prepared in the nursery for the park. At the base of the Round she had a fish-pond installed. The Lanhydrock steward wrote:

I have made arrangements for sending from Tehidy to Lanhydrock tomorrow about two dozen fishes as an experiment packed in wet grass – they will be sent in a gig from Truro & from thence by mail to Bodmin the same day – as they live for many hours in such a state I hope they will reach the pond alive.

Two weeks later, he wrote: 'The fishes sent from Tehidy, 51 in number all died before they reached the pond.'

(Right) The view from the house in 1833; watercolour by Charlotte Traherne

The parkland stretches away to the south-east into the valley of the River Fowey

What we see today is essentially a large-scale 19th-century planting, overlaying and extending the 17th-century core, rather than the 18th-century landscape so commonly found around English country houses. The 1st Lord Robartes continued his mother's vision by planting and replanting the woods to the north and west of the house as well as establishing the prominent plantations of Dreasonball, Colesloggett and Brownqueen – all forming key landscape features when viewed from the house and the High Garden. From the High Garden extensive views open up westwards over miles of country-side, once forming part of the estate. During the early 20th century the park was much used for recreation by the young family, including horse jumps, a swimming pool and even a mini-golf course, until bracken and fern eventually over-ran the park between the two World Wars.

The Parkland today

Today, the National Trust owns and manages 367 hectares (910 acres) of magnificent parkland, woodland, heathland and farmland as well as nearly two miles of the River Fowey. In 1999–2000 the Millennium Wood was planted, comprising 23,500 mixed broadleaved trees with a scattering of Scots pine. In time, this new woodland will provide a visual and sound buffer to the A30. Other new strips of woodland have been planted on land leased from Lanhydrock Farms. Designed to increase the thickness of the belts, these areas of new woods will eventually shield the gardens from the prevailing south-westerly winds. These shelterbelts suffered extensive damage during the 1990 hurricanes, but are now naturally regenerating.

On the far north-eastern edge of the estate was an area of unenclosed moorland formerly known as Lanhydrock Downs. Since grazing ceased on this area 60 years ago, scrub woodland has quickly taken over. More recently 4.5 hectares (11 acres) of scrub have been cleared to restore the area to heathland and it is grazed throughout the

The clean air encourages lichens and moss to flourish

summer by Dartmoor ponies. The parkland and farmland at nearby Cutmadoc are now farmed organically. The positive effects of this can be seen every spring, when the park erupts into a mass of wild flowers such as celandines, ladies smock, bluebell, pignut and bugle that provide an ideal habitat for a huge number of insects, which, in turn, become a plentiful food source for the rich birdlife and varied bat species. The estate is home to nearly every species of bat native to the UK, including the rare Barbastelle that lives under cavities in the bark of woodland trees. Many of the ancient trees on the estate have been mapped and are regularly monitored. They provide a superb habitat for many types of fungi, insects,

(Left) The rare dormouse thrives in the riverside woodlands

(Right) The beech and sycamore avenue

woodpeckers, nuthatches and owls. Trees that have fallen over take many decades to rot away, so are left or alternatively moved to a neighbouring tree clump to ensure a healthy structure to the woodland and provide an important link in the food chain.

The clean air in Cornwall along with the old open-grown parkland trees makes it an ideal place for many types of lichen to thrive. These grow on the bark of trees and are very sensitive to pollution, fertilisers and disturbance. The park is host to over 120 different species. If you look closely at the bark, you can see that the trees are totally covered and have an entirely different colour from trees of the same species nearer to towns and cities.

The River Fowey is home to dippers, kingfishers, all three types of woodpecker and the elusive otter. The river flows through some semi-natural ancient woodland that has carpets of wild daffodils every spring followed by a mass of bluebells. These riverside woodlands are also home to the rare dormouse that thrives amongst the hazel and bramble understorey entwined with honeysuckle. Each winter, riverside trees are coppiced to create 30-metre gaps alongside the banks. This gives a good uneven age-structure to the trees, stabilises the banks, and lets more light and warmth into the river, benefiting the invertebrates, salmon and sea trout.

The gardens and parkland are all open access, and there is a network of paths that lead you around. Many paths are flat and surfaced, which make them suitable for pushchairs and wheelchairs. A garden and estate walks leaflet is available with self-guided trails detailing horticulture, local wildlife and historical information.

The Robartes Family and Lanhydrock

The 17th century

Richard Robartes
'The wealthiest in the west'

The Lanhydrock estate was owned by the Glynn, Lyttelton and Trenance families from 1543 until *c.*1621, when the manor was acquired by Richard Robartes (*c.*1580–1634). Previous generations of the Roberts family (as they were then) lived in the Great House in Truro, which was demolished in 1960. Richard Robartes was celebrated as being the 'wealthiest in the west'. It was said that his father, John, had amassed a

Richard Robartes

fortune of £300,000 with 40,000 acres of land by the time of his death in 1614. Although much of this wealth was accumulated through supplying fuel for the tin industry, Richard became increasingly involved with the more dubious profession of money-lending, eventually being forced to pay £12,000 under threat of prosecution for usury in 1616. Despite this setback, he was keen to achieve a social status that matched his wealth. In 1614 he had become High Sheriff of Cornwall; two years later, he was created a knight, and in 1621 a baronet. Finally, in 1624 he bought the title of Baron of Truro from the Duke of Buckingham. This questionable deal was later broached during Buckingham's impeachment: 'that knowing Robartes to be rich he forced him to take that title of honour; and that in consideration thereof he paid £10,000 to the Duke's use'.

Sir Richard was living at Lanhydrock by 1626, when Hannibal Gamon delivered the funeral eulogy for his wife Frances in the adjoining church. (It referred to her house 'hereby' as distinct from 'her closset also of hers in Truro'.) A fine James I plasterwork panel dated 1621, which can be seen in the church, could well have come from the earlier house. Also from this earlier house came the present front door, which can be accurately dated to 1621–4.

John Robartes

Sir Richard's son John Robartes (1606–85), an Oxford-educated Puritan and, by 1634, leader of the Cornish Parliamentary Party in the House of Lords, had a far greater ambition to create a more imposing residence. Between 1634 (the date John succeeded his father) and 1651 (the date on the Gatehouse), the 2nd Baron substantially altered Lanhydrock to create an impressive, yet restrained mansion of four ranges round a central courtyard, incorporating his father's earlier manor house into what is now the north range. The completed house was similar in style to other provincial houses,

John, 1st Earl of Radnor

most notably Penheale House in Egloskerry near Launceston (*c.*1635) and Trewan near St Columb Major (1635).

John Robartes was married twice, first in 1630 to the staunch Puritan Lucy Rich (*c.*1615/6–46/7), youngest daughter of the Earl of Warwick, and second in *c.*1647 to her cousin Letitia Smith (*c.*1630–1714). The two ladies could not have been more different. Lucy was considered 'a precious comfort … one of whom the world was not worthy', while it was said that Letitia was flirtatious and 'shone at court with lustre'. When Robartes married for the second time he was 42 and his bride was 17. It was observed at the time that he was 'in love with her to distraction, and to complete her misery was a perpetual attendant on her person'. While Lucy gave birth to five children, Letitia produced fourteen.

John played an often-underestimated role in the political and theological debate of the day. His Puritanical principles led him to raise a regiment of foot in the name of Parliament that later fought at the battles of Edgehill and Newbury. In 1644 the Earl of Essex reported that the 'noble Lord Robartes by the sequestration of his estate and the plundering of his goods, and by the imprisonment of his children hath endured, he is now at length by the valour of his courage returned to his native home'.

His Cornish homecoming was brief. Robartes and an army led by Essex were forced south, fighting a final battle at Castle Dore near Fowey before fleeing by water to Plymouth. After a brief spell as Governor of Plymouth, Robartes, being a moderate Parliamentarian who favoured Parliament with monarchy, sought exile. As such, he staunchly opposed the execution of Charles I in 1649 as well as the concepts of military dictatorship and the subordination of the church. Disenchanted with Cromwell's Protectorate, he sought undisturbed retirement in Cornwall during the 1650s, when he completed the Gatehouse. By 1657 red deer were first contained within the park, and in 1664 a licence was granted to enclose 850 acres of deer-park spreading across three parishes.

After 1660, John Robartes, much favoured by the restored monarch Charles II, moved from Cornwall to Danvers House in London. Robartes was elevated to the Privy Council and became a very unpopular Deputy Lord Lieutenant of Ireland. In 1661 he became Lord Privy Seal and eighteen years later was created Earl of Radnor and Lord President of the Council, retiring in 1684.

Robartes's children shared their father's interest in scholarship and politics. The eldest son, Robert (1633–82), was an ineffective ambassador to Denmark, while both Hender (1635–88) and Francis (1650?–1718) were influential musicians, the latter becoming Vice-President of the Royal Society. All three were returned as Cornish MPs. Perhaps the most notorious of Robartes' children was Letitia (d. 1681), who was described by Pepys as 'a fine-skinned lady'. In 1679, against her father's wishes, she married the scurrilous playwright William Wycherley. The century drew to a close with a legal dispute raging between Wycherley and the 2nd Earl of Radnor over Letitia's estate, which was left wholly to the playwright. The case bankrupted Wycherley, who spent some time in debtor's prison.

The 18th century
'Neglect and decay'

The 2nd and 3rd Earls of Radnor

When the 18th-century traveller John Loveday visited Lanhydrock in 1736, he declared the house to be 'extremely out of repair and utterly destitute of furniture'. This is not surprising, as Charles Bodville Robartes (1660–1723), 2nd Earl of Radnor, Lord Lieutenant of Cornwall, MP and Fellow of the Royal Society, preferred his extravagant homes in St James's Square,

London, and at Wimpole Hall in Cambridge-shire. This latter house he inherited through his marriage to Elizabeth Cutler. The 3rd Earl, Henry (*c.*1695–1741), on coming into his inheritance promptly sold his uncle's fine collection of art and sculpture and, in 1724, ventured on a grand tour. Henry travelled throughout Europe and the Balkans before settling in Italy with a mistress, 'a singer lately on the stage in Naples'. His only visits back to England were to refinance himself in order to support his mistress, who, it was reported, 'does not care much what become of his person … but continues to touch his pence'. Another

Charles, 2nd Earl of Radnor

drain on his finances was his very large house in Venice, which he 'furnish'd most magnificently, for the use of a family brought with him from Naples'. Henry died in 1741 and like his uncle and great-great-grandfather before him was brought back to Lanhydrock for interment in the family crypt.

Mary Vere Robartes and George Hunt

With the failure of the direct male Robartes family line, the house and estate passed to the great-grand-daughter of the 1st Earl of Radnor, Mary Vere Robartes (d. 1758), and then to her eldest son, George Hunt (1720?–98) of Mollington Hall in Cheshire. The title meanwhile reverted to the grandson of the 1st Earl's second marriage, another John Robartes (1686–1757), who resided at Radnor House in Twickenham. The 4th Earl was the neighbour of the poet Alexander Pope and a great friend of the composer George Frideric Handel. He also amassed a great art collection that included the *Old Horse Guards, London, from St James's Park* by Canaletto. On the death of the 4th Earl, the Radnor titles became extinct.

The Cornish antiquary and naturalist William Borlase commented in 1758 that 'Everything in the house is in a state of neglect and decay'. Several years earlier Mary Vere had considered demolishing the house, writing to her son 'the house and furniture may well be worth £1,500 & sell for that if the house was pulled down'. Fortunately, this did not happen. The 1799 probate inventories show that George Hunt made substantial alterations to the house, sweeping away some of the Jacobean features such as the east-facing range and an interior chapel. He also brought in fine contemporary furnishings including Chippendale tables and Axminster carpets. However, in a

George Hunt in his uniform as an officer in the Cheshire yeomanry

fruitless attempt to make the granite walls more acceptable to the contemporary taste for red brick, he had the external walls painted red.

George Hunt was 'a gentleman of independent fortune', whose huge estate was very profitable and included many lucrative mineral rights. Such wealth brought political independence and allowed munificent benevolence to many good causes such as St Petroc's church in Bodmin. He never married and on his death in 1798 bequeathed the Lanhydrock estate to his niece, Anna Maria Hunt (1771–1861). Unfortunately, his will favoured his sister Mary Wilbraham's family, which left Anna Maria with a colossal debt that she slowly paid off, partially through sound estate management.

The 19th century
'A venerable old house'

Anna Maria Hunt

In 1798 Anna Maria, the granddaughter of Mary Vere Robartes, inherited the estate of Lanhydrock with its huge mineral reserves, an impressive, albeit ramshackle, mansion and a large, scattered estate. Over the ensuing 30 years she, along with her stewards William and Alfred Jenkin, transformed the fortunes of Lanhydrock.

Anna Maria had a very affectionate relationship with her mother Mrs Mary Hunt. They regularly visited the English spa towns together and shared a great affection for Lanhydrock. They spent much of their time in London, conveniently residing next door to one another in Mayfair. On 2 November 1804 Anna Maria married the successful London barrister Charles Bagenal-Agar (1769–1811), the youngest son of the 1st Viscount Clifden of Gowran Castle in Ireland. They had three children, Charles and Edward, who both tragically died in early

Anna Maria Hunt

childhood, and Thomas James (1808–82), who was to inherit the Lanhydrock estate. Charles Agar also died prematurely, from typhoid after only seven years of marriage, leaving Anna Maria as a widow for 50 years. She was buried alongside her mother, husband and two children in the chapel of St George's Fields Cemetery in London.

Over the years she was regarded as a 'conscientious and charitable landlord'. Her letters record her generosity towards starving miners during periodic slumps, and the benevolence shown to her tenants and staff as well as her business aptitude. She was astute in her financial investments and in profitable ventures such as canal building, industry, mining, property and loans to carefully vetted borrowers.

Anna Maria was a regular visitor to Lanhydrock. Such was her passion for Regency spa culture that she had sea water brought from Fowey to bathe in. She was also very aware of what we today regard as important conservation issues, installing Holland blinds in the picture galleries to prevent light damage, and stoves to combat dampness.

Thomas James, 1st Lord Robartes

Anna Maria encouraged her only surviving child, Thomas James, to adopt the Robartes arms and warrant in 1822, and when he came of age in 1829, he began to take some responsibility for the estate. His marriage in 1839 united two great Cornish families – the Robarteses and the Pole-Carews of Antony House. Although Juliana Pole-Carew (1812–81) was initially engaged to Sir William Molesworth of nearby Pencarrow House, she married Thomas James at St Marylebone in London close to his mother's home in Mayfair. Thomas James was MP for East Cornwall between 1847 and 1868.

In 1858 George Gilbert Scott was commissioned to carry out essential repairs to Lanhydrock House at a cost of £1,407 4s 6d. The work was entrusted to Scott's chief assistant and 'well tried man', Richard Coad, who supervised essential repairs to the house in 1857–64 as well as converting the old

Brewhouse into a Billiard Room and installing plate-glass windows. In addition, Coad oversaw the building of a new Coach House, most likely to Scott's design, and the laying-out of a new formal garden based on plans supplied by George Truefitt.

Thomas James's only son was Thomas Charles (1844–1930), who, in 1872, married Mary Dickinson (1853–1921) of Kingweston, near Somerton in Somerset, a lady of great warmth and dignity and fervent religious conviction. At the wedding in London the bride wore 'a white satin dress, trimmed with flounces of Brussels lace and wreaths of orange flowers, gardenias and stephanotis, with a veil and orange blossoms on her head'. She had twelve brides-maids. The couple honeymooned in Tunbridge Wells and Paris. Soon their first child, of an eventual ten, was expected.

(Right) Thomas James, 1st Lord Robartes
(Below) Lanhydrock in 1860

Lanhydrock on fire in 1881

Fire and restoration

'Not quite as bad as it seemed'

At around 1 o'clock on the afternoon of 4 April 1881 an exposed timber in the kitchen chimney caught fire. Fanned by a strong wind, the flames severely damaged the south range, while the roof of the west range was eventually lost, causing the inevitable collapse of historic plasterwork ceilings. The north range with its 17th-century Gallery survived, supposedly after dynamite was used to create a fire-break between the west and north ranges (although this seems unlikely). Within four hours of the fire breaking out, a telegram was sent to London: 'Lanhydrock on fire. Only the Gallery left. Lord and Lady Robartes well'.

Lord Robartes's only son, Thomas Charles, immediately returned from London to assess the damage. On 5 April he sent a telegram to his wife, saying 'Gallery is saved not quite as bad as it seemed to be'. Fortunately, Lanhydrock escaped total devastation. Despite much damage, the external and internal walls, the whole north range and half of the west range defied the blaze. Many would have considered it easier to demolish the fire-damaged Jacobean structure, but the instruction given by Lord Robartes was to reconstruct the house as it was prior to the fire, a restoration the architect described as 'in the spirit of conservation'. The positive news of Lord and Lady Robartes's health was short-lived: Lady Robartes died a few days after the fire, aged 68; Lord Robartes died the following year, reputedly of a broken heart.

Thomas Charles, 2nd Lord Robartes chose the Liskeard-born architect Richard Coad, by then with his own architectural practice, to

Architects – Richard Coad (1825–1900) and James MacLaren (1853–90)

Richard Coad was articled to the Liskeard architect Henry Rice, but soon moved to London to study architecture at the Royal Academy. He joined George Gilbert Scott's busy architectural practice in 1847, rising to the position of office manager, during which time Lord Robartes commissioned Scott to carry out repairs to the decaying mansion at Lanhydrock. In 1864–70 Coad acted as clerk of works for Scott's Albert Memorial in Hyde Park in London. During this contract Coad had set up his own architectural practice. In the 1870s Coad befriended the gifted Glaswegian James MacLaren and nominated him to study architecture at the Royal Academy.

The Lanhydrock commission caused Coad great anxiety; indeed, in 1882 he wrote, '[had] it been a new house my difficulties would have been far less'. As the contract went drastically over budget, tension arose between client and architect. Lord Robartes questioned payments amounting to £10,000 for the hot water, lead casements and fireproof ceilings alone. MacLaren added to Coad's problems, in 1884 telling Lord Robartes, 'I refuse to be associated with [Coad's] needless neglect'. Coad also failed to impress Lady Robartes, who turned to George Vialls and not Coad, when an architect was needed to restore the church in 1886. Despite such setbacks, Lanhydrock remains a fitting testament to the architectural proficiency of Richard Coad, the artistic flair of the young James MacLaren, and the skills of their High-Victorian craftsmen. Unfortunately, Coad's health declined drastically as a result of the Lanhydrock commission – he died in Battersea in 1900. MacLaren went on to become a leading light in the Art and Crafts and Aesthetic movements, but died aged only 37.

oversee the rebuilding of Lanhydrock. Furthermore, Lord Robartes insisted that the building contractors must be Cornish. Within days of the fire, Coad had produced an insurance estimate leading to an eventual payout of £12,350. Although Thomas Lang & Sons of Liskeard provided the winning tender of £19,406, the eventual cost of the restoration was £73,000. The sheer scale of the project was beyond Coad's resources, and so he took on a progressive young Scottish architect, James MacLaren, as his chief assistant. While Coad was responsible for the exterior and the engineering work, MacLaren focused on the interiors. The latter's eclectic contributions include the Aesthetic-style Dining Room, Elizabethan Teak Bedroom Stairs and Rococo Prayer Room chimneypiece. However, MacLaren's drawings make clear that the

prevailing style for the interiors was to be influenced by the fashionable Aesthetic Movement. To introduce such progressive interiors into a Jacobean setting was not unusual; rather, it would have been considered the height of fashion for a young progressive family.

(Right) The Agar-Robartes family about 1902

53

The 20th century
'A very kind and gentle family'

The family moved into the newly finished house in 1885, and for the next 30 years Lanhydrock was brimming with the enthusiasm and optimism of family life. Between 1879 and 1895 ten children were born to Thomas Charles Agar-Robartes and his wife Mary: one, John Radnor (b.1884), died after only six months. The century ended on a high note when Thomas inherited the Clifden viscountcy after an unexpected failure of the male Agar line.

The early 20th century was Lanhydrock's golden epoch. The house was packed with activity, entertaining notable Liberal party peers, who supported the eldest of the Victorian children, another Thomas (1880–1915), with his political campaigns in the county.

Tommy Agar-Robartes

Tommy, as he was affectionately known, was educated at Eton and Christ Church, Oxford, and was destined, albeit after initial reluctance, for a life in politics. (His father and grandfather had both been Liberal MPs before him.) With his good looks, sharp mind and enthusiastic personality, Tommy was elected to the south-east Cornwall constituency in 1906 as 'the Farmers and Miners Friend'. One month after his victory he was unseated for breaching electoral regulations. His high-profile case at Bodmin Assizes recorded 108 counts of bribery and other illegal behaviour, which included excessive expenses, illegal payments and a 'meat tea' for the estate workers that was considered 'a very extraordinary proceeding' by the presiding judge. Despite this, in 1908 Tommy was unopposed by the Conservative and Unionists for the mid-Cornwall (St Austell) division seat. His campaign was based on the support of Free Trade and temperance reform, while he regarded the principle of Hereditary Legislation as indefensible and injurious to the best interests of the democratic community.

In the lead-up to war in Europe, Tommy had passionately supported the growth of the Territorial Army and a strong military deterrent as 'a guarantee for the maintenance of Peace'. Indeed, Tommy himself was an officer in the 1st Royal Devon Yeomanry (Territorial Force) between 1902 until 1911. In February 1914 he drew up his will and six months later took an appointment as 2nd Lieutenant in the Royal Bucks Hussars. He was stationed in England, but 'could not bear the thought that others were taking risks which he did not share'. In February 1915 he left for France as an officer in the 1st Battalion Coldstream Guards and by June he had been promoted to captain. During the Battle of Loos in September 1915 Tommy was shot in no-man's-land and died in a field hospital shortly afterwards. On his death the *Cornish Guardian* reported: 'His Death was Grand, The Cause was Just.'

(Left) Tommy Agar-Robartes presenting the first reading of the Land Tenure Bill in the House of Commons; painted in 1907.

His mother wrote at Christmas 1915: 'We have had a terrible sorrow as our eldest son Mr Robartes died of his wounds in France in September, we hardly know how to bear our grief. I was simply devoted to him.' Three years later, she wrote, '[We] were a small party for Christmas as my 4 sons are still in France. We are thankful the fighting is over'. The loss of Tommy, as heir to the 70,000 acres of Cornish estate, was immeasurable. His youngest brother Alexander (1895–1930) received the MC, but never recovered from the psychological trauma of the war. He eventually jumped to his death from a window at the family's Belgrave Square home. Cecil (1892–1939) served in the Rifle Brigade, again to the detriment of his health.

Saving Lanhydrock

The First World War took a great toll on the family, but what happened next was unforeseeable. Of the surviving eight children, only two married and from those marriages only one child was born: Rachel, daughter of Major Victor Agar-Robartes, later 8th Viscount Clifden. Another setback for the family was the uncertain future of agriculture, which prompted large-scale land sales during the second decade of the 20th century. After the Second World War,

with Rachel living in Africa, the future of Lanhydrock was uncertain. The family must have seen only too clearly the potential threat of demolition once again. It was the historical importance and visual impact of the park rather than the splendour of the house that secured the future of Lanhydrock with the National Trust. Indeed, in 1953 Lord Esher, then chairman of the National Trust Historic Buildings Committee and friend of the 6th Viscount Clifden, insisted that the house was 'incidental' to the surrounding landscape. In 1953 the house and 400 acres were given to the National Trust by Gerald (1883–1966), 7th Viscount Clifden, who, until his death, continued to live in the house with his two spinster sisters, Everilda (1880–1969) and Violet (1888–1965). In 1974, on the death of the 8th Viscount, the title became extinct. The Williams family, descendants of the 8th Viscount's only daughter Rachel, still live locally and continue to farm in the area.

With the last members of the family still resident, six rooms within the house opened to visitors in 1954. By the mid-1980s Lanhydrock was attracting 85,000 visitors per year. Twenty years later, our visitor figures passed 200,000, making it one of the most popular historic houses in the country.

(Right) Gerald Agar-Robartes, later 7th Viscount Clifden, in 1927 by W.B.E. Ranken

(Far right) Violet Agar-Robartes in 1926 by W.B.E. Ranken (From the Family Museum)

The Lanhydrock evacuees

'We will never forget our stay at Lanhydrock, and the many kind people who gave so much of themselves to a lively bunch of children.'

Pauline Castle, 2000

Of all the good causes which Gerald, 7th Viscount Clifden and his two sisters espoused, the most interesting was the hospitality they offered a group of evacuee children from London. Violet attended their arrival at the Lanhydrock Village Institute and brought back seventeen children, instead of the intended ten. Her kindness and endearing nature was reflected in her comment, 'Well you couldn't just leave them'. For a few dramatic years, these children became the new family at Lanhydrock House.

At an evacuee reunion held at Lanhydrock in 2000, Daphne Woosnam commented:

It was really remarkable when you think they had no experience of children. I can see Miss Violet now with the dogs at her heels and children hanging on her arms and a basket and we'd all go up to the kitchen gardens…. Miss Violet was always involving herself with our activities, … and in the summer time, treats were organised, outings to the seaside. I well remember us all setting out; the old Rolls driven by Mr Baker, the Austin (8 or 10) driven by Mr Odgers, and following on the pony Jingle, with Miss Violet and the big girls. I remember we walked up hills to give the pony a breather.

Anita Burgh, the daughter of a member of the house staff and today a celebrated novelist, recalled:

When Miss Everilda or Miss Violet had to make trips they would often take a couple of the children with them for a treat. I adored that huge Rolls-Royce, the squishy well worn seats, the smell of it. A glass window separated us from the driver; instead it had a speaking tube which they let us use for amusement. There was a cocktail cabinet, devoid of alcohol, of course, and a picnic basket. Our legs were always covered by plaid travelling rugs. I fared better than my sister who was always carsick and had to sit in the front while I was indulged in the back. We went everywhere, to Mevagissey, to Padstow, once to Mousehole. Most years there was a picnic at Dozemary pool and we stopped for tea at Jamaica Inn.

Daphne remembered how both sisters encouraged the evacuees to read:

Miss Violet found that I particularly liked to read historical romances and she took me to her room and over her bed she had this bookshelf, I think the whole works of Charlotte M. Yonge and I could borrow them one by one. Each time we took one back we used to have a little chat about it. What do you think of this? What do you think of that? What was interesting about this book?

You had this feeling, looking back now, that Lanhydrock as a whole welcomed us. It was as if everyone gathered round the House, with all the children. There was this sort of rapport between everybody… We had the best of upstairs and down-stairs. We had the staff, who were our friends and also the Robartes.

The evacuees' bedrooms were situated in the Nursery Wing. It was a shock for some of the evacuees when the National Trust took over, many felt that they had lost the personal family link with the house. Since that time, however, they have largely enjoyed the regeneration of the house and joined in its success in recent years.

(Right) The evacuees performing a nativity play in the village hall. Lord Clifden is on the left